Tawny Owl

By Ruth Owen

Educational Consultant:
Dee Reid

Tips for Reading with Your Child

- Set aside at least 10 to 15 minutes each day for reading.

- Find a quiet place to sit with no distractions. Turn off the TV, music and screens.

- Encourage your child to hold the book and turn the pages.

- Before reading begins, look at the pictures together and talk about what you see.

- If the reader gets stuck on a word, try reading to the end of the sentence. Often by reading the word in context, he or she will be able to figure out the unknown word. Looking at the pictures can help, too.

- Words shown in **bold** are explained in the glossary on pages 22–23.

Above all enjoy the time together and make reading fun!

Book Band Blue

For more information about tawny owls go to:
www.rubytuesdaybooks.com/wildlifewatchers

What do you know about tawny owls?

How can you tell a bird is a tawny owl?

- It has red and black feathers.
- It has blue and yellow feathers.
- It has brown and white feathers.

What is a baby owl called?

- An owlet
- A toddler
- A twit-ta-woo

Where does an owl family live?

- In a garden shed
- In a tree trunk
- On a boat

What do baby tawny owls eat?

- Eggs
- Mice and frogs
- Seeds and berries

Now read this book and find the answers.

It is night in the woods.

A tawny owl sits in a tree.

He sees a mouse on
the ground.

The owl flies down.

talons

He grabs the mouse with
his **talons**.

The owl brings the mouse back to his nest.

The mouse is food for his **mate**.

He calls to her.

Hoo hoo hoo hoooo

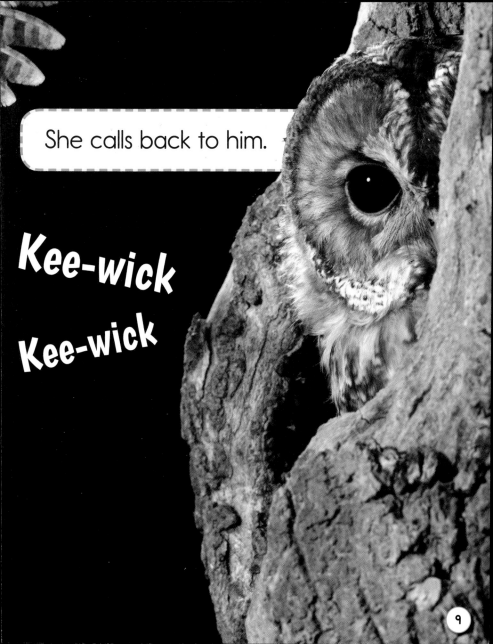

She calls back to him.

Kee-wick
Kee-wick

The nest is inside a tree trunk.

tawny owl egg

The female owl has laid two eggs in the nest.

She keeps the eggs warm.

nest hole

She can't leave the eggs,
so the male brings her food.

After 30 days, two little **owlets**
hatch from the eggs.

owlet

frog

The mother and father owls hunt for food for the owlets.

The mother owl rips up the food for the owlets to eat.

a four-week-old owlet

When the owlets are
four weeks old they leave
the nest.

The little owlets can't fly, but
they can walk and climb.

The mother and father owl bring the owlets food to eat.

mother owl

a six-week-old owlet

A six-week-old owlet can eat a mouse all in one go!

An owl eats all of a mouse.

It eats its bones and fur.

Then the owl sicks up
the bones and fur.

This is called an
owl **pellet**.

owl pellet

fur

bone

The owlets learn to fly and hunt.

a 12-week-old owl

All the owls hunt at night.

When they are 20 weeks old the owlets leave their mother and father to begin their grown-up life.

Glossary

mate
An animal's partner with which it has babies.

owlet
A baby owl.

pellet

A tightly packed lump of unwanted bits that an owl sicks up after eating.

talons

Sharp claws used for hunting by birds such as owls and eagles.

Tawny Owl Quiz

1. How does a tawny owl catch a mouse?

2. How many eggs did the female owl lay?

3. What is happening in the picture on page 13?

4. What happens when an owl swallows bones and fur?

5. Which picture in the book did you like best? What is happening in the picture?